FAUN

by Vinnie H̶ ̶ ̶ ̶ ̶n̶

SAMUEL FRENCH

Copyright © 2023 by Vinnie Heaven
Cover design by Ciaran Walsh at CiwaDesign
All Rights Reserved

FAUN is fully protected under the copyright laws of the British
Commonwealth, including Canada, the United States of America, and all
other countries of the Copyright Union. All rights, including professional
and amateur stage productions, recitation, lecturing, public reading,
motion picture, radio broadcasting, television, online/digital production,
and the rights of translation into foreign languages are strictly reserved.

ISBN 978-0-573-02401-6

concordtheatricals.co.uk
concordtheatricals.com

FOR AMATEUR PRODUCTION ENQUIRIES

UNITED KINGDOM AND WORLD
EXCLUDING NORTH AMERICA
licensing@concordtheatricals.co.uk

020-7054-7298

Each title is subject to availability from Concord Theatricals,
depending upon country of performance.

CAUTION: Professional and amateur producers are hereby warned
that *FAUN* is subject to a licensing fee. The purchase, renting, lending
or use of this book does not constitute a licence to perform this title(s),
which licence must be obtained from the appropriate agent prior to any
performance. Performance of this title(s) without a licence is a violation
of copyright law and may subject the producer and/or presenter of such
performances to penalties. Both amateurs and professionals considering
a production are strongly advised to apply to the appropriate agent
before starting rehearsals, advertising, or booking a theatre. A licensing
fee must be paid whether the title is presented for charity or gain and
whether or not admission is charged.

This work is published by Samuel French, an imprint of Concord
Theatricals Ltd.

No one shall make any changes in this title for the purpose of production.
No part of this book may be reproduced, stored in a retrieval system,
scanned, uploaded, or transmitted in any form, by any means, now
known or yet to be invented, including mechanical, electronic, digital,
photocopying, recording, videotaping, or otherwise, without the prior
written permission of the publisher. No one shall share this title, or part
of this title, to any social media or file hosting websites.

The moral right of Vinnie Heaven to be identified as author of this work has been asserted in accordance with Section 77 of the Copyright, Designs and Patents Act 1988.

USE OF COPYRIGHTED MUSIC

A licence issued by Concord Theatricals to perform this play does not include permission to use the incidental music specified in this publication. In the United Kingdom: Where the place of performance is already licensed by the PERFORMING RIGHT SOCIETY (PRS) a return of the music used must be made to them. If the place of performance is not so licensed then application should be made to PRS for Music (www.prsformusic.com). A separate and additional licence from PHONOGRAPHIC PERFORMANCE LTD (www.ppluk.com) may be needed whenever commercial recordings are used. Outside the United Kingdom: Please contact the appropriate music licensing authority in your territory for the rights to any incidental music.

USE OF COPYRIGHTED THIRD-PARTY MATERIALS

Licensees are solely responsible for obtaining formal written permission from copyright owners to use copyrighted third-party materials (e.g., artworks, logos) in the performance of this play and are strongly cautioned to do so. If no such permission is obtained by the licensee, then the licensee must use only original materials that the licensee owns and controls. Licensees are solely responsible and liable for clearances of all third-party copyrighted materials, and shall indemnify the copyright owners of the play(s) and their licensing agent, Concord Theatricals Ltd., against any costs, expenses, losses and liabilities arising from the use of such copyrighted third-party materials by licensees.

IMPORTANT BILLING AND CREDIT REQUIREMENTS

If you have obtained performance rights to this title, please refer to your licensing agreement for important billing and credit requirements.

FAUN was co-produced by Cardboard Citizens, Alphabetti and Theatre503. The show premiered on 28 March, 2023 at Alphabetti Theatre. The cast was as follows:

ACE ....Aitch Wylie (they/them/he)
PAIGE/DOE .... Nyah Randon (she/they)
ANT/STAG/PLANT ....Afton Moran (they/them)

Writer – **Vinnie Heaven (they/them)**
Director – **Debbie Hannan**
Assistant Director – **Pia Richards-Glöckner (she/they)**
Movement Director – **Chi-San Howard (she/her)**
Designer – **Jacob Lucy (he/him)**
Lighting Designer – **Laura Howard (they/she)**
Sound Designer – **Mwen**
Sound Associate – **Nat Norland (they/them)**
Production Manager – **Tabitha Piggott for eStage (she/her)**
Stage Manager – **Chloe Astleford (she/her)**
Interim Stage Manager – **Livvy Lynch (she/they)**
Dramaturg – **Emma Williams**
Costume Co-Designer – **Sophia Khan**
Production Electrician and Relighter – **Ariane Nixon**
Interim Relighter – **Ash Copeland**

Citz Futures Trainees

Wolf D. Knox-Hooke
Ra'eesah
Jamie T

FAUN toured the UK between 28 March - 13 May 2023, visiting Newcastle, London, Plymouth, Birmingham, Salford and Bristol. Tickets were available at £1 or on a 'pay what you feel' basis through the tour to people with experience of homelessness and poverty.

FAUN was supported by the Citz Futures Traineeship; providing paid opportunities for people without significant prior work experience and with experience of homelessness, inequity, or poverty to gain hands-on experience of working in theatre alongside industry professionals. Three trainees for *FAUN* were placed in a variety of backstage and production roles, with support from across the creative team.

Cast

AFTON MORAN | Ant, Stag and Plant

Afton Moran (they/them) is a nonbinary actor based in Edinburgh, Scotland. They hold a BA (Hons) in Drama and Performance from Queen Margaret University.
Theatre credits include; *Special Agent M in Happiness Collectors* (The Audio Story Company), Afton in *Sex Education Xplorers* (Independent Arts Projects), Francesco Del Cosa in *How To Be Both* (R&D, Royal Lyceum Theatre), *Right Brain in Brain Matter* (Imaginate), *8:8* (Mercimax/Swiss Arts Council).
Film/TV/audio credits include; Narrator in *Not Seeing Straight: Celebrating Queer Art and Lives* (National Galleries of Scotland), Angus in *68 Months in Waiting* as part of Scenes For Survival (National Theatre of Scotland/BBC), Pan in *Ghost Light* (National Theatre of Scotland), *What I Know Now* (BBC Social).
Nominated by The National Theatre of Scotland for the Evening Standard's Future Theatre Fund Award.

AITCH WYLIE | Ace

Theatre includes: *Alice's Adventures in Aerialand* (Open Bar Theatre); *Our Last First* (The Union); *Snowflake: A New Musical* (The Lowry); *Stages: A Video Game Musical* (Vaults); *The Phase* (workshop); *The Three Musketeers* (UK Tour).
Audio includes: *Dr Who: The War Master* (Big Finish) Russell T Davies' *Dark Season* (Big Finish)

NYAH RANDON | Paige and Doe
Nyah is from West London and started their artistic training at The BRIT School studying musical theatre. She has recently graduated with a degree from Fourth Monkey. Also a writer, Nyah uses their own experiences with the aim of celebrating the world around her. In 2020, they created a short film which has been selected and awarded by festivals. She has travelled, loves swimming in open water, is a strong singer and mover who plays the flute and reads tarot.
Screen credits include: *Enola's Tape; Bill Nye Saves the World; Sylvie; Looked Like You*; and the music video *Falling*.
Previous stage credits include: *Variant 31; Signed Sealed Delivered - A Stevie Wonder Tribute; The BRIT Awards; The X-Factor; Just So; Fame; One Sun One World; Swanning Around; and Musicians of the Future.*

Creative Team

VINNIE HEAVEN | Writer

Vinnie is a writer and actor, their plays include: *She's a Good Boy* (UK tour 2019) and *Charmane* (UK tour 2019). Their acting credits include: *The Nevers* (HBO), *MO <3 KYRA 4EVA* (Film4), *The Misfortune of the English* (Orange Tree Theatre), *The Living Newspaper* (Royal Court) *Cuckoo* (Soho Theatre.) and *PowerOut* (BBC).

DEBBIE HANNAN | Director

Debbie is a director and writer for stage and screen with a focus on new work. They are Associate Director at National Theatre of Scotland and were formerly Acting Artistic Director at Stockroom. Previously Associate Director at Bunker Theatre, their credits include: *Sound of the Underground, Pah-Lah* (Royal Court); *Exodus, Panopticon* (National Theatre of Scotland); *The Strange Undoing of Prudencia Hart* (Manchester Royal Exchange); *Overflow* (Bush Theatre); *The Ugly One* (Tron Theatre); *Cuckoo* (Soho Theatre); *Little Miss Burden* (Bunker); and *Constellations* (Donmar). They recently directed a short for Film4 and 104 Films, co-written with Matilda Ibini, and are writing their first feature.

JACOB LUCY | Designer

Theatre includes: *Dead Air* (Stockroom); *Purple Snowflakes and Titty Wank* (Royal Court & Abbey, Dublin); *The End of History* (St Giles-In-The-Fields); *The Enchanted* (Bunker); *Brixton Rock* (The Big House). As co-scenographer, theatre includes: *Neverland* (Parco Corsini, Italy).

LAURA HOWARD | Lighting Designer

Laura is a Lighting Designer originally from Croydon. They graduated in 2020 from LAMDA's Production and Technical Arts course and were a recipient of the William and Katherine Longman Charitable Trust Scholarship.
Assistant Lighting Designer credits include: *Amadigi* (English Touring Opera); and *Constellations* (Donmar/West End).
Lighting Designer credits include: *The Beach House* (Park 90); *The Kola Nut Does Not Speak English; Elephant* (Bush Theatre); *Manorism* (Southbank Centre); *Clutch* (Bush Theatre); *Exodus* (National Theatre Scotland); *Invisible* (Bush Theatre); *Juniper & Jules* (Soho Theatre); *Dead Air* (Stockroom); *Moreno* (Theatre503); *SPLINTERED* (Soho Theatre); *Cell Outs* (Camden People's Theatre); *We Never Get Off At Sloane Square* (Drayton Arms); *SHUGA FIXX vs The Illuminati* (Relish Theatre); *curious* (Soho Theatre); *The Moors; Three Sisters; I Hate it Here; Sparks; Nine Night; The Laramie Project* (LAMDA).

MWEN | Sound Designer

Mwen has been working creatively with sound as an artist, producer, composer, DJ and session musician for a number of years. More recently Mwen's creative output expanded to include sound design and composing for theatre, live performance and film. Mwen's creative practice melds the worlds of music technology, electronic music, live sound and performance. Mwen's compositions and productions have received airplay on BBC Radio 1, BBC Radio 6, XFM, NTS, Rinse FM, been supported by DJs including Rob da Bank, Mary Anne Hobbs and Tom Robinson and synced to TV and fashion film. Currently, Mwen is based in London and DJs regularly on the London club scene. Mwen is also in-house Ableton tutor at Hub16 Studios in East London and a tutor at The Institute of Contemporary Music Performance (ICMP).

SOPHIA KHAN | Costume Co-Designer
Sophia is an experienced wardrobe supervisor, WHAM (Wig hair and makeup artist), afro hair consultant and facilitator. She started her creative career working as a dresser and then wardrobe HOD for live music shows, which was the catalyst for her career working with bands and musicians including; George Michael, Lady Gaga, Dolly Parton and Motorhead. She has also worked in the ice-skating industry, touring globally with a variety of different live shows and subsequently moving into theatre.
In recent years Sophia has held workshops teaching, The History and importance of Afro Hair in TV, Theatre and Film. She is also a WHAM consultant, specialising in afro hair and deeper skin tones and holds workshops on this topic for sound and lighting departments.

CHI-SAN HOWARD | Movement Director

Theatre credits include: *Les Miserables* (Sondheim Theatre, UK Tour, Netherlands/Belgium Tour); *Betty! A Sort of Musical* (Royal Exchange); *O, Island* (Royal Shakespeare Company); *Ivy Tiller: Vicar's Daughter, Squirrel Killer* (Royal Shakespeare Company); *A Midsummer Night's Dream* (Shakespeare North/Northern Stage); *The Narcissist* (Chichester Festival Theatre); *Chasing Hares* (Young Vic); *That Is Not Who I Am/Rapture* (Royal Court); *Corrina, Corrina* (Headlong/Liverpool Everyman); *The Taxidermist's Daughter* (Chichester Festival Theatre); *Anna Karenina* (Sheffield Crucible); *Two Billion Beats* (Orange Tree Theatre); *Aladdin* (Lyric Hammersmith); *Milk and Gall* (Theatre503); *Arrival* (Impossible Productions); *Typical Girls* (Clean Break/Sheffield Crucible); *Glee and Me* (Royal Exchange); *Just So* (Watermill Theatre); *Home, I'm Darling* (Theatre by the Lake/Bolton Octagon/Stephen Joseph Theatre); *Harm* (Bush Theatre); *Living Newspaper Ed 5* (Royal Court); *Sunnymeade Court* (Defibrillator Theatre); *The Effect* (English Theatre Frankfurt); *The Sugar Syndrome* (Orange Tree Theatre); *Oor Wullie* (Dundee Rep/National Tour); *Variations* (Dorfman

Theatre/NT Connections); *Skellig* (Nottingham Playhouse); *Under the Umbrella* (Belgrade Theatre/Yellow Earth/Tamasha); *Describe the Night* (Hampstead Theatre); *Fairytale Revolution, In Event of Moone Disaster* (Theatre503); *Cosmic Scallies* (Royal Exchange Manchester/ Graeae); *Moth* (Hope Mill Theatre) *The Curious Case of Benjamin Button; Scarlet; The Tempest* (Southwark Playhouse); *Adding Machine: A Musical* (Finborough Theatre)

Film credits include: *Hurt by Paradise* (Sulk Youth Films); *Pretending* - Orla Gartland Music Video (Spindle); *I Wonder Why* - Joesef Music Video (Spindle Productions); *Birds of Paradise* (Pemberton Films).

TABITHA PIGGOTT | Production Manager

Tabitha Piggott is a production manager for eStage working in theatre and opera, with a particular passion for new writing. She studied Production and Technical Arts at LAMDA as a Leverhulme Arts Scholar and was production manager on Papatango and Bush Theatre's Olivier Award winning Old Bridge in 2021.
Credits include: *All of Us, Barrier(s), Connections 2022* (National Theatre); *Only an Octave Apart* (Wilton's Music Hall); *Paradise Now!, Favour, Red Pitch, Old Bridge, Overflow* (Bush Theatre); *Fefu and her Friends* (Tobacco Factory Theatres); *Raising Icarus* (Birmingham Rep); *Winner's Curse, The 4th Country* (Park Theatre); *The Boys are Kissing, Moreno* (Theatre503); *The Dancing Master* (Buxton Opera House).

CHLOE ASTLEFORD | Stage Manager

Recent credits include: *The Suppliant Women & The Egyptians* (Gulbenkian, Canterbury); *Polunin's Romeo & Juliet* (Royal Albert Hall), *Alice In Wonderland* (Brixton House); New English Ballet Theatre's Summer season (Royal Opera House, Cheltenham Everyman, The Grange); *Counting Sheep* (Vaults, Waterloo); *Madam Butterfly* (Cadogan Hall); *Dead Air* (Riverside Studios); *The Hive* (Hoxton Hall); Director's Showcase (Drama Centre London); Housemates Festival (Brixton House); *Nell Gwynn* (Mountview); *Syllable* (Trinity Laban, Bonnie Bird Theatre); *Tempus Fugit* (Union Theatre); and *A Midsummer Night's Dream* (East London Shakespeare Festival, outdoor tour). Chloe also works regularly on cabarets at the Windmill Theatre, Soho.

PIA RICHARDS | Assistant Director

Pia Richards is a theatre maker, occasional performer, disability and youth arts advocate. Pia gained a lot of her experience as a young person participating and performing with Company Three and eventually going on to work at Company Three and the Barbican Centre. Since she has worked in various support roles, working with theatre writers and doing

Access Support work with disabled artists, helping to disassemble
barriers that make working in the arts difficult. She has also been
working as an Assistant Director on *Juniper and Jules* (Soho Theatre).

EMMA WILLIAMS | Dramaturg

Emma creates performances for diverse audiences working
collaboratively across art forms. Her roles range from Director,
facilitator dramaturg and writer. She has regular co-created shows for
South West based companies Green Ginger, Pickled Image, Opposable
Thumb Theatre and Vic Llewelyn. Emma has created in house
productions for The Tobacco Factory Theatres, Bath Theatre Royal, The
Bristol Old Vic and The Wardrobe Theatre. Her writing credits include
The Desert Daydreamer for Royal Welsh College of Music and Drama
and *The Kings* for Popelei Theatre company.

Theatre503 is at the forefront of identifying and nurturing new voices at the very start of their careers and launching them into the industry. They stage more early career playwrights than any other theatre in the world – with over 120 writers premiered each year from festivals of short pieces to full length productions, resulting in employment for over 1,000 freelance artists through their year-round programme.

Theatre503 provides a diverse pipeline of talent resulting in modern classics like *The Mountaintop* by Katori Hall and *Rotterdam* by Jon Brittain – both Olivier Award winners – to future classics like Yasmin Joseph's *J'Ouvert*, winner of the 2020 James Tait Black Prize and transferred to the West End/BBC Arts and *Wolfie* by Ross Willis, winner of the 2020 Writers Guild Award for Best New Play. Writers who began their creative life at Theatre503 are now writing for the likes of *The Crown*, *Succession*, *Doctor Who*, *Killing Eve* and *Normal People* and every single major subsidised theatre in the country now boasts a new play by a writer who started at Theatre503.

Theatre503 Team

Artistic Director	Lisa Spirling
Interim Executive Director	Jules Oakshett
Literary Manager	Steve Harper
Producer	Ceri Lothian
General Manager	Tash Berg
Carne Associate Director	Jade Lewis
Literary Associate	Lauretta Barrow
Trainee Assistant Producer	Tsipora St. Clair Knights
Technical Manager	Misha Mah
Marketing Officer	Millie Whittam
Administrator	Lizzie Akita
Development Coordinator	Heloise Gillingham

Theatre503 Board

Erica Whyman OBE (Chair), Royce Bell (Co-Vice Chair), Eleanor Lloyd Emma Rees, Jack Tilbury, Luke Shires, Ollie Raggett, Roy Williams OBE Zena Tuitt

Theatre503's work would not be possible without the support of the following individuals, trusts and organisations:

We are particularly grateful to Philip and Christine Carne and the long-term support of The Carne Trust for our International Playwriting Award, the 503 Five and Carne Associate.

503Patrons

Berlin Associates, Caroline & Tim Langton, Cas & Philip Donald, Catharine Roos, Céline Gagnon, David Baxter & Carol Rahn, DavidsonMorris Solicitors, Eilene Davidson, Eric Bensaude, Erica Whyman, Freddie Hutchins & Oliver Rawlins, Gaskell & Jennifer Jacobs, Geraldine Sharpe-Newton, Ian Mill KC, Jack Tilbury/Plann, Lisa Swinney, Lou Wilks & Tom Gowans, Louise Rawlins, Marcus Markou, Marianne Badrichani, Matthew Marren, Nick Hern Books, Pam Alexander & Roger Booker, Robert O'Dowd, Sean Winnett, Steve Winter, The Bell Family, The Bloor Family, Tim Willcox, United Agents and all our 503Friends and Share the Drama supporters.

503Slate Supporters

Cas & Philip Donald, Concord Theatricals, Eilene Davidson, Gordon Bloor, Jean Doumanian, Kater Gordon, Kofi Owusu Bempah, Royce Bell.

Arts Council England Grants for the Arts, Backstage Trust, Battersea Power Station Foundation (Right to Write), Cockayne Grants for the Arts (503 Productions), Concord Theatricals (503 Playwriting Award), Garrick Charitable Trust, Noel Coward Foundation (Rapid Write Response), Theatres Trust, The Foyle Foundation, The Orseis Trust (503Five), Wandsworth Borough Council, Wimbledon Foundation (Five-O-Fresh).

Alphabetti Theatre

Alphabetti Theatre is an award winning, artist led performance space in Newcastle upon Tyne, formed by Ali Pritchard in 2012. Alphabetti Theatre is a gateway for new artists, writers and performers find the stage and has given artists their first playing stage.

They believe great art should be for everyone, regardless of financial situation. And that's why forty-three percent are being charged at Pay What You Feel, with the remaining fifty-seven percent being ticketed. They average three hundred performances, supporting one thousand two hundred and fifty artists & welcoming thirteen thousand five hundred audience members.

In the past three years they've produced, commissioned, created or co-produced eighty-nine publicly funded projects. These funders include: Arts Council England, National Heritage Lottery Fund, Community Foundation, Newcastle City Council, Women's Centenary Fund, The Prince's Trust.

Alphabetti Theatre Team

Artistic and Executive Director – **Ali Pritchard**

Executive Assistant – **Claire Overton**

Venue Producer – **Esther Fearn**

General Managers – **Sam Johnson and San Persaud**

General Supervisor – **Sunny Howlader**

Community Engagement – **Audrey Cook**

Marketing Coordinator – **Scott Jeffery**

Technical Coordinator – **Chris Foley**

Alphabetti General Assistants – **Nic Freeman, Maya Torres, Rosie Bowden, Elijah Young, Réka Szalkai, Keiran Wadforth, Siobhan McAuley**

Associate Producers – **Eilis McGowan, Gina Rffin, Chloe Stott**

Associate Literary Manager – **Ben Dickenson**

Theatre Dog – **Rex**

Alphabetti Theatre Trustees

Jon Fathering

Janet Plater

Joanne Hodson

Ruth Patterson

Alphabetti Theatre is supported by Arts Council England Grants for the Arts, Community Foundation, Garfield and Western, National Lottery Fund

Cardboard Citizens

Cardboard Citizens creates theatre with, for and about people with lived experience of homelessness, poverty or inequity. We use theatre, art and training to empower individuals to make change in their own lives, and in their communities.

We run a Membership programme for people with experience of homelessness or living in poverty, offering free workshops, information, advice and guidance, training and qualifications and creating opportunities for employment in the theatre industry and beyond. We create theatre rooted in issues of poverty, homelessness and the inequity which causes them, working with artists who speak from experience and creating performances in both theatres and in hostels, prisons, and community venues. Through the stories we tell, we seek to create positive change in audiences, across the arts sector, and in wider society. Cardboard Citizens is supported by Ambassadors Kate Winslet CBE, David Morrissey and Rory Kinnear. Over the past three decades, Cardboard Citizens has garnered critical and public acclaim for outstanding theatre that puts the stories of people with lived experience of homelessness in the spotlight. Chris Sonnex was appointed Artistic Director, our first production under his leadership was *Bangers*, performed at Soho Theatre following a tour to hostels and community venues in 2022.

Cardboard Citizens was founded by Adrian Jackson MBE in 1991, past productions directed by Jackson include *The Ruff Tuff Cream Puff Estate Agency*, produced in partnership with the Belgrade Theatre and Coventry UK City of Culture; the critically-acclaimed *Cathy; Bystanders* at the Edinburgh Fringe; *Home Truths* at the Bunker Theatre; the Evening Standard Award-winning *Mincemeat*; *Pericles* and *Timon Of Athens* (with the RSC); *The Beggar's Opera* (with ENO); *The Lower Depths* (with London Bubble) and *A Few Man Fridays*.

www.cardboardcitizens.org.uk
Twitter: **@CardboardCitz**
Facebook: **facebook.com/CardboardCitizens**
Instagram: **@cardboardcitz**

Cardboard Citizens staff

Membership Manager – **Rachel Jessica Angeli**
Executive Director & Joint CEO – **Lisa Briscoe**
Youth Engagement Manager – **Aliyah Forde**
Director of Development & Communications – **Katherine Harding**
Executive Assistant – **Jessica Hutchinson**
Finance Manager – **Nasima Khanam**
Director of Programmes – **Flora Newbigin** (maternity leave)
Marketing Manager – **Vicky Ream**
Development Manager (Individuals & Corporates) – **Leone Richmond**
Executive Producer – **Clare Robertson**
Artistic Director & Joint CEO – **Chris Sonnex**
Producer – **Jack Wakely**
Head of Engagement – **Jessie Wyld** (maternity cover)

Board

Chair – Prue Skene CBE
Vice Chairs – Jenique McNaught, Matthew Xia
Treasurer – Chris Bull
Marcus Bernard
Ayesha Casely-Hayford
Charlie Josephine
Ajeet Jugnauth
Sacha Milroy
Jon Opie

HELP SUPPORT THE WORK OF CARDBOARD CITIZENS

Cardboard Citizens has been producing theatre with, for, and about people affected by homelessness since 1991, and expanded our mission in 2022 to include those affected by poverty or inequity. From our base in Whitechapel, London, Cardboard Citizens delivers a programme of performing arts workshops to develop skills and wellbeing as well as provide vital information, advice, and guidance. The company reaches fifteen hundred homeless and at-risk individuals each year.

Each year Cardboard Citizens must raise over £1 million to deliver outreach, educational and artistic programmes of work. It is only as a result of your support, that we can assist, advise and empower more people than ever before in the years to come.

To support Cardboard Citizens' work, you visit **cardboardcitizens.org.uk/donate** to make a regular or one-off donation. Thank you for your support.

This production and our Citz Futures Traineeship programme are supported by Arts Council, England Project Grants, Cockayne Foundation, Evan Cornish Foundation, Foyle Foundation, The Linbury Trust, The London Community Foundation and Societe Generale UK Foundation.

CHARACTERS

ACE – They/He – Trans-Masculine, Nonbinary, early twenties. Charming to the point of people pleasing. Secretly sarcastic and line by line becomes drier in tone rather than earnest.

PAIGE – She/Her – Cisgender female, early twenties. Social media marketer, high status, bold and strong. Loves candles and tea and is pretty good at doing life.

ANT – He/Him – Cisgender male, mid twenties. A bar manager who likes video games. He is a loveable idiot. Kind and gentle to the best of his abilities.

DOE – They/She – Early thirties. Blunt and honest, says it how it is. Takes all who need support under their wing and fiercely defends them. Practices tough love because they know that life requires it.

STAG – He/They – Early thirties. Softly masculine with lashings of femme. We don't know if we want to be them or be with them. A pair of glitter antlers and a dazzling glitter beard. High heels and probably a cape. A comic. Sarcastic and thinks on his feet. They ooze charisma. A born master of ceremonies.

PLANT – A giant plant with pleasing leaves like a Monstera/Calathea type. Comforting but poised to be cheeky. Big enough to both hug a person and give them a good, necessary slap.

AUTHOR'S NOTES

The cast where possible should consist entirely of Trans/Nonbinary/ GenderQueer actors. This play is an opportunity to let trans artists shine, casting a broad spectrum of trans and nonbinary existence is a must. The cast should reflect the diversity of the world.

Notes on the text

The cast should resist the temptation to play the suffering: these characters speak about hard things in light ways and use humour to cope.

When faun parts are referenced they are similar visually to that of a baby deer. The full transformation of Ace should resemble a Faun, the mythical half human half deer/goat creature, but in this case very much deer and not goat! They should always have a human face. The same for Doe and Stag, they have the antlers and ears etc of deer but remain half human at the same time. No character is ever fully an animal.

This play was written for three actors to multi-role but could be performed by up to six.

When alone Ace speaks directly to the audience.

Text in **bold** indicates an aside during a conversation that is spoken directly to the audience.

"/" indicates a character being interrupted.

ACKNOWLEDGEMENTS

Thank you to Chris, Clare and the whole team at Cardboard Citizens for commissioning and delivering this play. Thanks to Alphabetti and Theatre503 for giving these words a home.

Thanks to The Outside Project for their help with early research. Thanks to Zachary Hing and Reece Lyons for your creative in-put on early drafts.

A massive thanks to the cast; Afton, Aitch and Nyah, for offering all of your beautiful selves to this project.

Thanks to the team; Jack, Jacob, Laura, Mwen, Chi-San, Tabitha, Chloe, Pia, Sophia, Nat, Livvy, Alex, Ra'eesah, Wolf and Jamie.

Thank you to Jamie Lee for encouraging my writing for so many years.

Thanks to Kit Spoonsy Springer for your endless and unwavering love and support.

Thank you to Emma Williams, for your love, guidance and encouragement. Thanks for telling me that I am good enough. Sorry that someone once thought you were my Mum in a corner shop in Oxford, I know you hated that, luckily no one else knows... Anyway, I hope to never be without your creative wisdom.

Thank you to Debbie Hannan for lending your immense talent to this play, I am honoured to have your name attached to it. Thank you for your resilience, your brilliance and constant support. Thank you for teaching me the power that imagination holds and for using mine to re-build me. You truly dazzle me. My love is on you.

This is dedicated to Bash, who taught me that life is magic and for living!

One

(The edge. This is a liminal space that sits between two worlds, the world that contains the house share and the world of the Queer Forest. A large IKEA bag sits in the middle, it is clearly on neither side, but between.)

*(From inside the IKEA bag appears **ACE**, twenty-two, Trans Masculine. On the top of their head is a pair of small, velvety fawn like antler nubs.)*

(They step out of the bag and stretch, deer like, it's quite pleasing to watch.)

(They directly address the audience.)

ACE. It's cramped in there. I get sore glutes.

(They shake their hips about for some relief. They notice a new tail.)

Ugh.

(They feel it.)

Great.

I'm as confused as you are.

I'm Ace, twenty-two, Leo sun, Aquarius moon, intuitive, creative, risk-taker – but I'm said to be more like double Libra...a peace keeper. Bet you were thinking Capricorn, because of the – clear personal ambitions but no.

ACE. I'm sofa surfing – currently – just for now – only at the moment. I've actually just sorted out the next one, it's Sofa number thirteen. It's Paige and Ant's sofa. A straight couple.

Now, sofa owners are delicate creatures, skittish. You need to lure them in. Like a horse with a sugar cube. A sugar cube for example, in the form of a small succulent – three for one pound. Flat palm, extended, calm voice, some compliments – your hair looks great, love your shoes, speaking of, mine are already off, ready for your sumptuous carpet. Reassure them – put them at ease, talk casually about the importance of cleanliness in communal areas. Watch for subtle changes in their behaviour, a nose huff grows in to an eye roll, grows in to, um I just need the living room back, my sister is visiting.

Always know you've outstayed your welcome before they do. This is key.

Now there might be some cis-hets amongst us who I should say at this point can probably skip the next step here. But for my fellow queers, listen up. An offer of someone's sofa to stay on does not mean instant equality is being gifted. In situations of precarity you're going to need to smile, not too much, that's creepy. You need to be ready with your please and thank yous. They want gratitude from us, so excessive gratitude must be provided. You should always feel like you're on the edge of a curtsey. There's no room for embarrassment, mould on the walls? no problem, cockroach? they're older than the dinosaurs, they deserve to be here, leak in the ceiling? no really, thank YOU. Trust me on these, I'm a pro.

Now, if you mess up – panic – really panic – But remember you can't go wrong with cheap ingredients for a fancy meal, half price wine and a big old grin. Charm not smarm – that's what you need.

(From the Queer Forest there is a sound. It startles **ACE** *– they peer fearfully in to the forest before snatching up their bag.)*

So, cue the charm not smarm offensive.

Here goes...

(The doorbell to the house appears, glowing. **ACE** *remembers their tail and nubs just in time. They tuck the tail in and whack a hat on.)*

Two

(The house.)

(This is a house share setup. The living room has one of those cheap, chunky, black leather sofas that they all seem to have. It's worn out and yet somehow still spectacularly solid and uncomfortable. On a side table sits a giant three wick candle that for all we know will burn for eternity, or at least until the tenancy is up.)

*(**PAIGE** is stuffing an old pillow in to a pillow case.)*

*(**ANT** is in the way, no matter where he moves. He is trying to get an ancient hoover to turn on.)*

PAIGE. It's too late now, I've said they can/

ANT. /this hoover stinks.

PAIGE. They'll be here in/

ANT. /It smells cheesy, don't you think?

PAIGE. Because you hoovered up coffee Ant. You got it wet, on the inside, and then just left it to get gross.

ANT. I think you should maybe email the landlord about it.

PAIGE. I/

ANT. /actually don't, in case she wants to do an inspection and she finds Ace here.

PAIGE. You're okay with it then?

ANT. Is that my bottom pillow?

PAIGE. I don't know, I just grabbed one.

ANT. Its mine. I can tell from the stains.

    (**ANT** *reclaims his pillow.*)

PAIGE. I didn't want to say this. I didn't. But I pay more towards the rent, don't I? And I'm saying he's staying.

ANT. G won't like it.

PAIGE. G has been in the living room once in a whole year – and that was only because she was confused.

She won't care. She's like, never here – which I get, because she lives in a box room at thirty-two – depressing.

ANT. By thirty-two I'm gunna have a two-bed house in Camden and a sausage dog, probably called like, Midnight Beast or Warren.

PAIGE. As I was saying, Ace won't be here long.

ANT. Warren the midnight beast! He'll have all the bitches drooling.

PAIGE. It's just like a stop gap type thing.

ANT. Yeah but people always say that just to get a foot in the door. Then a year later we'll be sat here vibing three abreast, thinking, well this is shit.

PAIGE. Three abreast? *Abreast?*

    (*The doorbell goes.*)

ANT. Paige, we're already in a house share without also having to hold someone who's life is in crisis, it's just long.

    (*The doorbell goes again.*)

PAIGE. It's fine. You'll survive.

ANT. I just don't want any bad vibes, I feel like we're getting back to a good place and this could/

PAIGE. Not now Ant –

(**ACE** *appears.*)

Ace! Oh my God it is so good to see you. Welcome, welcome. Would you mind taking your shoes off/

(**ACE** *is one step ahead.*)

ACE. Way ahead of you. Not that I think I'm better than you. I don't, because I'm not.

PAIGE. Okay then...

Aww It's been so long, we need a proper catch up.

(**ANT** *is subtly dazzled by* **ACE**.)

ANT. *(Hyper-masculine.)* Hey mate, Ant *(Offering his hand.)*

ACE. Ace.

ANT. He him, *(Winks.)* you?

ACE. Oh, uh, they, them, he, him.

PAIGE. I already told you that Anthony.

ANT. I know. *(To* **ACE**.*)* But it's nice to be asked isn't it.

ACE. Sure.

(To the audience.) **It's not.**

PAIGE. We can get the rest of your stuff in.

(They leave momentarily. **ACE** *takes in the room and the old sofa.)*

ACE. **Is it me or does it smell cheesy in here?**

*(**PAIGE** and **ANT** return – there is no other stuff.* **ACE** *only has one bag.)*

This is all *so* great. Look at this place, love it. That sofa, wow.

It looks like they made it without removing the cow from the leather.

ANT. Is this all you've got?

ACE. Sorry, I should have said. Yeah, just – just this.

PAIGE. Is the rest still at your Mums?

ACE. Yeah.

ANT. Wait, so you do have a Mum and all that?

PAIGE. Anthony.

ANT. You can't live there? Too small? Or don't get on or something?

ACE. Something like that.

Nothing like that.

ANT. I'm sure you'll make up mate.

ACE. Mm.

We won't. I did a tiny shit in all her commemorative royal tea pots.

ANT. Positive attitude.

ACE. Yeah, definitely.

Including the Princess Diana one.

ANT. If it was me I'd give her a call, take charge of the situation, have it out.

PAIGE. Ant that's enough, go and sort some drinks or something, you're upsetting them.

ACE. No, that's okay, you're good. Honestly. It's fine.

ANT. We're all good, see.

*(He holds **ACE** who is clearly uncomfortable.)*

ACE. I bought you a succulent.

> (*They produce a shit looking cactus in a small glittery pot.*)

PAIGE. That's so cute, thank you. Aww, it's so small.

ACE. **Told you, works a treat.**

PAIGE. I've made up the sofa for you.

ACE. Looks perfect, thanks – so, so comfy.

   And my tears will roll straight off.

PAIGE. Just try not to puke wine down the back of it like you did at my eigthteenth.

ACE. Oh no, don't. I bet you still hate me after that.

ANT. So *that's* why your Mum doesn't allow drinks in the lounge.

PAIGE. No, I think that's just because she doesn't like you.

ANT. I'm not good enough, apparently she'd be better off with some dickhead banker.

PAIGE. Instead of a dickhead bar manager.

   Joking baby.

> (**ANT** *doesn't take it well and busies himself.*)

ACE. Thanks for this Paige. I'm – look, I'm, really – embarrassed – that I'm having to do this, and, I – I am one hundred percent going to stay out the way, keep everything tidy, keep the noise down.

   I'm grateful to you guys, I honestly have tried everywhere else that I could.

ANT. So will you be in a lot do you think or?

PAIGE. Stop talking.

It's going to be so fun having you here. The only thing we wanted to say, was that like, we get things are pretty shit for you right now but we obviously have our own life stuff as well and –

ACE. Oh yeah, yeah, yeah, I totally respect that. I absolutely won't, I won't, pile all my shit on to you or anything.

ANT. Cool.

ACE. I don't even have any shit, to be honest.

I left it all in my Mum's tea pots.

This is just a shortage of money thing.

PAIGE. You don't have to explain.

ACE. No, right, yeah, I just want to reassure you that I'm all good. I'm actually manifesting getting some more shifts and finding a cheap room – and that is actually meant to work.

PAIGE. Yeah? Good for you. Put your stuff under the sofa or on the drinks trolley bottom shelf.

Oh, and G lives in the box room, second door on the left, next to the bathroom.

ACE. Got it. Thanks.

PAIGE. She's not very social.

ACE. **Lucky her.**

PAIGE. She lives off toast and never wipes up the crumbs.

ACE. **A loner and a criminal, well, well.**

PAIGE. A few weeks a year she makes shit flans and sourdough because *Bake Off* is on.

ACE. Fair enough.

PAIGE. Also she can get quite aggy if you use her things.

ACE. Right.

ANT. Gluten free flour is expensive, apparently.

PAIGE. So don't be like G.

ACE. Privileged? Couldn't be if I tried mate!

Yeah, God, no.

ANT. Do you lift?

ACE. *(Confused.)* No.

ANT. I'll teach you. It'll be sexy.

ACE. ...will it?

ANT. Two topless bro's – lifting. That'll be lit.

ACE. Great! Let's do it!

I'd rather die.

PAIGE. We're picking up pizza Ace, you want some?

ACE. Uh-nah. I'm okay. Money.

PAIGE. I guess we could/

ACE. /No. No, you've done enough – too much if anything.

PAIGE. We'll see you in a bit then, if you need anything just text me okay.

ACE. I won't, you definitely won't hear from me.

> *(They leave. ACE is alone. A beat of stillness. Listening for G upstairs, nothing. They take a tiny branch out of the bag and slowly nibble off the leaves.)*

I said I was good at this... I didn't say it was easy.

Three

(The house. Morning. There is a tranquil feel to the living room. Birdsong drifts in, sun beams hit the floor. ACE has a moment to breathe a sigh of relief.)

(Then.)

(PAIGE flies through the door taking them by surprise, they scream.)

PAIGE. No screaming before nine am.

ACE. Sorry. Morning.

A screaming curfew? Is that a thing?

(ACE springs in to action clearing up the space.)

PAIGE. Central line delays and I need to be in before nine.

(ACE is trying to stay out the way.)

ACE. Sorry, am I in your way? Are we okay after the screaming? Are you annoyed at me?

PAIGE. I'd already forgotten about it, don't stress.

I literally can't be late today, I'm starting a massive campaign.

ACE. I'm sure you'll be fine. Just move that stuff if you need.

PAIGE. Severe Delays. Severe.

ACE. I'll get out your way.

PAIGE. This could affect your journey in as well.

ACE. Oh I've been walking in, so I'm okay.

PAIGE. You're so lucky.

ACE. **It takes over an hour.**

I don't have a shift today anyway. The café's dead at the moment/

PAIGE. I'm going to have to get my boss to delay the client.

It's Misty Lake.

ACE. Not heard of it, sorry.

PAIGE. Misty Lake, the new personalised candle shop.

ACE. Oh right!

Sounds shit.

PAIGE. It's in Shoreditch.

ACE. I don't really buy candles.

I don't have money to literally burn.

PAIGE. You should, you get to pick the colour and the scents and then they mix it for you. It's so good. Its where I got the bathroom one – the bergamot and sweaty sex.

ACE. Oh cool.

Eww.

PAIGE. Maybe I can Uber. This is pissing me off, do you know how many people in grad positions get this kind of opportunity?

ACE. **I didn't go to uni, so no, no I don't.**

PAIGE. It's like none, it's pretty much just me.

ACE. How much digital marketing does a candle shop need?

PAIGE. Everyone needs digital marketing Ace. Everyone.

ACE. Right.

PAIGE. Ugh, I can't leave yet, I haven't even had a tea. This is too much.

Actually – could you like, maybe make me one whilst I sort my bag out?

> (*A feeling of, what the fuck, but* **ACE** *is on the last sofa...*)

ACE. Of course. I should have offered you one.

PAIGE. Thanks Ace, love you.

ACE. *(Tentative.)* Could I maybe have one as well?

PAIGE. Not you trying to get free shit when you've already got my sofa.

ACE. **Biiitch.**

PAIGE. Joking, have one.

ACE. **I take it back.**

PAIGE. But buy the next box yeah?

ACE. **Biiiitch.**

Absolutely.

PAIGE. Could you maybe/

ACE. Empty the bin? Was just about to, it stinks right?

PAIGE. Ant just lets it stink for days. Idiot.

ACE. Your shoes are – nice. Whole outfit looks – great.

PAIGE. Thank you.

Tea?

ACE. On it.

PAIGE. And there's toast crumbs all over the side again!

ACE. Think that's G – but I'll sort it no worries.

> (*They leave.*)

Four

(The house.)

*(Its two am, **ACE** is asleep, a mound of blankets. Loud crying and wailing starts. **ACE** wakes up and grumpily wraps himself in the blanket to drown out the noise.)*

(The wailing continues.)

*(**ANT** returns home from his bar shift. He is a little bit pissed. He clomps his way in and oblivious sits down on top of **ACE**.)*

ACE. Sorry to bother you there Ant –

ANT. Shit!

ACE. Was just wondering if you needed the room or if I could sleep?

ANT. Sorry mate, one too many after my shift, forgot you were there.

ACE. No worries.

ANT. We had a cheeky little lock-in.

ACE. I think Paige is crying upstairs. Maybe you should go and check on her?

    *(**ANT** listens.)*

ANT. Nah, that's G.

ACE. Should we see if she's okay?

ANT. Nah, she does that every now and then. She's fine.

ACE. Terrifying.

Does she often do it in the early hours of the morning?

ANT. Yeah. She probably doesn't want to disturb anyone.

ACE. She's directly above me.

ANT. Yeah but technically this doesn't count as a bedroom.

ACE. **Stinger!**

ANT. Sad really.

Move over then let's play *Halo*!

ACE. Could you maybe play it upstairs?

ANT. How? The TV is in here.

> (**ANT** *scoops them up, blankets and all.*)

(In a stupid voice.) Come on grumpy – play with me.

> (**ACE** *wriggles free.*)

ACE. *(Light-hearted.)* That sounds like you want me to touch you inappropriately.

ANT. Woah, there is clear PS5 context here. You filthy nugget.

ACE. **Filthy nugget?**

Sorry. I'm really tired.

ANT. No you're not. It's the morning now anyway.

Grab the other controller.

Oh my God, guess what! Ferret guy was in the bar again tonight. Totally different ferret on the lead though…less bite-y.

ACE. Are you really going to sit and play that? I can't tell if you're joking.

ANT. *We* are going to sit here and play it.

ACE. **A classic cis-het power move.**

ANT. Come on!

ACE. I'm not really in to computer games, I'm pretty bad
at them.

ANT. My ex-boyfriend used to say that. But he loved them
eventually.

> (**ACE** *gives the audience a look of – he's
> queer?!*)

We actually used to play this after we'd been at it.

ACE. **So, I've actually seen his outline in grey joggers,
when he did "no pants Sunday" and let's just say it's/**

ANT. Impressive isn't it.

ACE. What?!

ANT. The graphics.

ACE. Oh.

It's two am. I want to scream.

I should leave you to it, head out, late night walk...or
something.

ANT. Staaay, it will be a laugh.

Paige never lets me play – it's two am or never. Come
on mate. I like spending time just me and you.

ACE. No me too – yeah.

(Lying.) I actually enjoy just *watching* games. So, I
could do that.

ANT. Sweet. I streamed on Twitch for a while. Had around
eighty followers...made affiliate. Don't want to brag.

ACE. Amazing. I'll just curl up at this end and put this
over me to block out the light a tiny bit.

> (**ACE** *curls up under a blanket.*)

ANT. I've got some beers in the fridge, you want one?

(**ACE** *appears out the blanket, a fresh set of fawn's ears have sprouted on their head.*)

ACE. Two am beers...perfect.

(*They feel the ears and panic.*)

I have to – I'm going to have to – stretch my legs...'cus I have cramp...in my, calves? I better walk really fast, out of here, okay bye.

(**ACE** *runs out.*)

ANT. Ace wait, I'll go upstairs – Ace?

(*He turns the game off, disappointed and a little rejected, he heads upstairs.*)

Five

(The edge. ACE stands between the two worlds, back where they began their story.)

ACE. I've got ears – more ears, I've got ears above my ears!

Oh Christ, what is happening?

The nubs, then the tail, now this.

(They exhale deeply.)

Get a grip Ace.

I have to keep it together. I cannot mess this up!

(They panic again.)

But this is weird, this is not good, what is this?!

(They start to frolic a little bit, they stamp like deer do, raising one leg slowly then stomping it down – this builds a bit until they are thrashing about and getting it all out.)

(In doing so they accidentally step over into the Queer Forest, the mood changes.)

(They see small billows of smoke rising, as though someone is chain smoking deep within.)

(The distant sound of a drone and some ominous deep singing*.)

---

* A licence to produce *Faun* does not include a performance licence for any third-party or copyrighted music. Licensees should create an original composition or use music in the public domain. For further information, please see the Music and Third-Party Materials Use Note on page iii.

(Afraid. They slowly place a foot back over the line and in to the safety of the edge before leaping their whole body over. Safe but scared.)

The house is fine. The house is great. I love the house.

Hide the ears, hide the nubs. Go back to the house.

Six

(The house.)

(A Friday night, music, alcohol, laughter, togetherness*.)

*(**ACE** has their faun ears and nubs very well hidden.)*

PAIGE & ANT. *(Chanting.)* ONE MONTH! ONE MONTH! ONE MONTH! WOOO!

ACE. Why is this a celebration?

Yeeeaaaaahhhh!

PAIGE. Should we be celebrating you being here for a month already?

ACE. No.

PAIGE. I mean, probably not. But it's an excuse to get high. So, here's to our disgusting little throuple.

ACE. I've prepared something for you both actually, as a sort of thank you – for letting me crash here. I just want you to know that you're awesome, both of you, thank you.

PAIGE. You don't need to thank us, it's chill.

ACE. I wanted to. I know it's not the easiest set up with me here

I'm lying, I'm literally the perfect housemate.

And to be honest I really needed a distraction so it was good for me.

---

* A licence to produce *Faun* does not include a performance licence for any third-party or copyrighted music. Licensees should create an original composition or use music in the public domain. For further information, please see the Music and Third-Party Materials Use Note on page iii

ANT. That's cute.

ACE. Thank you.

A distraction from being the only one who empties the bins and having to do G's washing up for four weeks.

PAIGE. What is it then? Let's see.

ACE. Okay. Right.

> (**ACE** *produces a set of panpipes and prepares for the performance. The panpipes should have the aesthetic of a flute from Greek Mythology, like the one first used by the God Pan who constructed it out of reeds.*)

PAIGE. (*Quietly to* **ANT**.) What the actual hell...

> (**ACE** *plays a basic melody,* **ANT** *and* **PAIGE** *aren't moved but are respectful.*)

> (*As* **ACE** *gets more lost in the music they do small leaps and frolics, the perfect faun, skipping in moonlight, in crispy winter evening air.*)

> (*This state moves in to something more gnarly, a concert is appearing, lights, lasers, haze, the melody becomes a well-known pop song, a big hit that everyone would know. This is getting cooler*.*)

---

* A licence to produce *Faun* does not include a performance licence for a specific song. The publisher and author suggest that the licensee contact PRS to ascertain the music publisher and contact such music publisher to license or acquire permission for performance of the song. If a licence or permission is unattainable for that song, the licensee may not use the song in *Faun* but should create an original composition in a similar style or use a similar song in the public domain. For further information, please see the Music and Third-Party Materials Use Note on page iii.

(A platform rises from the floor elevating
ACE *as he starts to Panpipe beatbox.)*

*(***PAIGE*** *and* ***ANT*** *watch, wide eyed.)*

(The music continues, the leaps, the bounds,
it is way beyond the realms of imagination
now. There are disco balls. Then the giant
three wick candle suddenly bursts in to life!
Three giant flame thrower flames reaching
up to the ceiling. Is this Cirque de Soleil!?
ACE *is themselves now the panpipes, a giant*
dancing set of wooden pipes with little legs.
Now they themselves are the music, they
sing out the panpipe anthems which grow
more emotional, lights closing in, piano
accompaniment, tears and phone torches
waving. They scatter flower petals over **ANT**
and **PAIGE** *and massage their heads. This is*
for them after all.)

(The fading of the surreal. The bleeding back
in to the real moment, in the small living
room, with the old chunky black sofa. **ACE**
stands rigid with nerves, eyes wide and
awkwardly puffing in to a panpipe, like a
child in a talent contest. The reality is that
they were kind of shit at it. They blow the last
two notes.)

*(***PAIGE*** *and* ***ANT*** *look to each other then back*
at **ACE**. *They are silent.)*

ACE. They're probably just emotional. Overwhelmed
by the beauty. Dazzled...probably.

(They don't know what to say. **ANT** *clears his*
throat then speaks as if to a child.)

ANT. Well done you. That was –

PAIGE. Sweet. That was sweet of you.

ACE. I'm so glad you liked it.

>   *(A beat.)*

ANT. When did you start learning to...uh...play it?

ACE. I just got in to it recently actually, not sure why.

ANT. Do you reckon you'll keep it up or –

ACE. Imagine how good I'll be with more practice.

PAIGE. *(To stitch up* **ANT**.*)* I'm away with work next week so you can practice it all you like then.

ANT. Well, I'll still be here/

PAIGE. Shall we get back to the party then?

ACE. Yes!

>   PAAARRTTYY TIIMMMEEE!

>   Was that too loud? Sorry about that.

>   *(Music, drinks, fun*.*)*

---

* A licence to produce *Faun* does not include a performance licence for any third-party or copyrighted music. Licensees should create an original composition or use music in the public domain. For further information, please see the Music and Third-Party Materials Use Note on page iii.

Seven

(The house. The morning after. Silence.)

*(**ANT** and **PAIGE** are intertwined on the sofa. They slowly stir. Too bright. Too painful.)*

*(From out of the IKEA bag appears **ACE**, dazed and confused, they were sleeping in there.)*

(The following overlaps completely with hysteria. There is a real sense of togetherness, being equal and sharing space.)

PAIGE. No, I actually can't/

ACE. /I can't even explain/

ANT. /I'm calling you Billy Bookcase/

ACE. /What's happening here/

PAIGE. /that has killed me off, literally, I'm dead/

ACE. /I guess I live in here now/

ANT. /You're like a futuristic turtle/

PAIGE. /Please, I need to see if I would fit in there.

ANT. /I didn't know you came from Norway mate/

ACE. /I think IKEA is Swedish/

(In a micro second of silence.)

ANT. Show us your meatballs!

(A beat. Awkward.)

Dunno why I said that...

(Laughter.)

PAIGE. It's cute all being down here together, we should do it more.

ANT. It's cold in here though.

PAIGE. We need to get a heater can't have you being cold at home.

ACE. **A heater, get in! You're witnessing a masterclass.**

PAIGE. *(Small wretch.)* I need water.

> (**PAIGE** *leaves.*)

ANT. Oooft, last night! You were hilarious.

ACE. Hopefully not too annoying?

ANT. Annoying? Nah, total opposite.

(A little shy.) You're brilliant.

...loud though.

ACE. Oh God.

ANT. I don't know how Paige slept through your karaoke.

ACE. Oh. God.

ANT. Luckily, I loved it though! And thanks for the chat... and for listening. I appreciate it.

ACE. **No memory.**

Of course mate, any time.

> (**ANT** *smiles, they fist bump.*)

I'm nailing this, thank you drunk me. Can't get cocky though, must maintain the charm.

> (**PAIGE** *returns.*)

How are you feeling?

PAIGE. I think I might be sick.

> No wait.

> I think I need food.

> Sick.

> No?

> It's hunger pain.

ACE. I'll make breakfast. Pancakes all good?

ANT. Pancakes. Yes. Good.

PAIGE. I've got yoghurt and fruits in the fridge.

ACE. Perfect, I'll whack them on top.

> Have you also got flour, eggs and milk?

PAIGE. Don't think so.

ANT. I'll go get some. I will save us all!

> *(He trips and stacks it onto* **ACE**. *They linger with each other a little too long,* **ACE** *clearly waiting for* **ANT** *to move.)*

PAIGE. Get Sprite as well please.

> *(***ANT** *jumps up.)*

> *(Flustered.)*

ANT. Okay bye.

Eight

*(The house. A different day. **ACE** has a blanket over their lap, hands hidden within it, their head is back and there is a look of euphoria on their face. **ANT** comes in, clocks them.)*

ANT. Oh damn, bro, are you?

ACE. I thought you were out.

ANT. Clearly.

> *(**ANT** sits beside him. Absolutely loving this.)*

Don't mind me.

> *(**ACE** is frozen.)*

I'd never even considered you cracking one out in here.

ACE. *(Embarrassed and trying to save face.)* What? – no/

ANT. /Oh you so are.

ACE. *(Hyper-masculine.)* I'm so not.

ANT. I'm being rude I should give you privacy.

ACE. I'm not/

ANT. But it is funnier to watch you die inside.

ACE. I'm not wanking!

> *(**ACE** produces a share bag of crisps. **ANT** is horrified.)*
>
> *(Beat.)*

ANT. The posh crisps.

ACE. I'll replace them.

(A tiny head shake to the audience to say, no I won't.)

ANT. You must have a death wish.

ACE. Its just crisps.

ANT. Just crisps would be prawn shells, or cheese puffs, these are baked not fried.

ACE. She won't know.

ANT. She always knows!

ACE. I'll apologise.

ANT. Can't apologise if you're dead!

ACE. Is it that bad?

ANT. It's the worst thing you could have done.

ACE. Worse than using her razor?

ANT. Her ray – wait for where?

ACE. Huh?

ANT. Back, crack, cheeks or sack?

ACE. Well not sack obviously...

ANT. Cheeks or crack then?

ACE. I'll get new ones.

ANT. Oh yeah, you can afford Waitrose yeah?

ACE. These are Waitrose?

ANT. Yeah, they are buddy. And not the basic range either.

ACE. No?

ANT. You've done it now. They're probably eight pounds per crisp! And that razor is Venus Comfort-Glide, so you better start saving.

You should have had a wank instead.

ACE. I really should.

ANT. It's not too late.

ACE. What?

ANT. I can just turn the TV up and not look.

ACE. Bro!

>   (**ACE** *whacks him with a cushion.*)

ANT. Calm down, it's alright, she thinks the razor was G. Because like me she didn't imagine you dragging it over your peach fuzz.

ACE. Thanks for that.

ANT. You look stressed. You should do something to release the/

ACE. /I'm not going to touch myself Ant.

ANT. What if I touched myself?

ACE. I would punch your dick off.

ANT. He's tougher than you think. How do you think he lost an eye?

>   (**ANT** *does a penis impression closing one of his eyes and straining his head forwards, they both laugh.*)

(*Light-hearted.*) Do you ever steal any of my stuff?

ACE. **Steal?**

ANT. Well...?

ACE. I don't steal stuff. I wanted crisps and I couldn't be bothered to go out. She's been away all week, she won't even notice.

ANT. Do you eat my Petit-Filous?

ACE. No.

ANT. Pepperami?

ACE. No.

ANT. Haribo?

ACE. No.

ANT. Quiche?

ACE. I don't eat your food.

ANT. The evidence suggests otherwise mate.

ACE. **I've had it before, the thief label, it's insulting.**

ANT. I would get it, I just want to know.

ACE. **I hate getting angry, it makes my nubs itchy.**

ANT. I probably would, in your shoes.

ACE. **Charm not smarm, charm not smarm, CHARM NOT SMARM.**

> (**ACE** *grins manically.*)

ANT. Desperate times and that...

ACE. **Why is it that people always assume that you did something deviant to end up like this – sofa surfing I mean – not the head nubs.**

ANT. Scuttling about here like a borrower, scoffing down custard creams. Hey, we should set up camera traps, catch you in night vision stealing shit in the early hours like a magical woodland creature.

> (**ACE** *is insulted and snaps.*)

ACE. You're all the same you lot. Can't quite see us as human, can you? I don't steal food! I have a job Ant, I work, I would work a hell of a lot more if I had the option to but – it's hard – it's different for *you* –

Steal your quiche? If I want a quiche then I'll buy a shitting quiche.

Me being here, this, this is because I am trying – trying to – It's insulting to be called a thief.

This sofa and this bag, it's all I have, that's it – why would I risk losing it for a bloody – I don't take things – quiche?!

I'm just – ugh! – I'm making choices for my safety. *You* wouldn't ever understand that.

I don't even know where to start because what you just said is so shitty! I can't even –

I just sleep on your sofa Ant. That doesn't make me a thief. I just sleep on your sofa. Like how you sleep in your bed.

> (**ACE** *itches the hell out of their velvety nubs.* **ANT** *has a silent moment taking in what was said.*)

Shit, I've fucked it.

ANT. *(Sincerely.)* Look, I apologise. I was really out of order. I'm upset that I've upset you.

ACE. No, I'm sorry.

I can save this.

I don't know what happened there. You're such a nice guy. I'm a prick. Sorry. You must hate me now.

ANT. You had every right/

ACE. /I'm sorry, I'm sorry, so sorry.

ANT. I'm sorry.

> (*There is a long moment. It should be long enough to hold* **ACE**'s *relief, fear and regret and* **ANT**'s *genuine processing of what he has heard. There is a moment where* **ANT** *is shifted and where he has to say that –.*)

ANT. I say stupid things because I like you. You somehow make me act like a wanker because I want to impress you.

>   (**ACE** *is confused.*)

ACE. Oh.

ANT. Do you – like *me*?

ACE. You're Paige's boyfriend.

ANT. Those were Paige's crisps.

>   (*Beat.*)

ACE. Good point.

>   (*They make out.*)

>   (**ACE** *enjoys an epic shag, controlling it and extracting every inch of pleasure from it. Wild and free. But* **ANT** *is falling in love, slow and soft, silk pyjamas and champagne, he melts.*)

Nine

*(The morning after the night before. **ANT** and **ACE** are curled up together under a heap of blankets. **ACE** is the first to wake.)*

*(**PAIGE** appears, coat on and suitcase in tow. She's back early. Very early.)*

PAIGE. Knock, knock, you decent?

*(**ACE**'s head spins.)*

Sorry it's so early. I got an earlier train. I'm just sneaking through to the kitchen, I'm going to take Ant a little surprise breakfast in bed.

*(**ACE** holds **ANT** under the blankets to avoid him appearing. **PAIGE** throws her bag on the sofa and goes through to the kitchen.)*

ACE. No problem. You look great today.

(Quiet panic.) Ant, Ant.

*(**ANT** stirs awake, oblivious.)*

You need to go upstairs, right now.

ANT. *(Sleepy.)* You want to do it in my bed? – Filthy.

ACE. Ant! Paige is home early.

ANT. Huh?

ACE. She's in the kitchen, she thinks you're upstairs.

ANT. Oh God. Okay, well we need to tell her, so let's just get it out the way.

ACE. Don't joke right now, go upstairs.

ANT. I'm not joking.

ACE. Ant.

ANT. I *really* like you, I think I could –

> (**ACE** *is in panic.* **PAIGE** *appears, to see the two of them sitting there, she takes in the scene in complete silence.* **ACE** *is a deer in the headlights, huge eyes sweeping from one person to the other.*)

> (*More silence.*)

PAIGE. Are either of you going to say anything?

> (**ANT** *nods and preps to be the barer of bad news.*)

ACE. *(Panic, stalling.)* What do you want us to say?

PAIGE. Sorry, maybe? Or, explain?

ANT. Babe, hear us out and this won't be as bad as it seems.

ACE. Because nothing has happened.

PAIGE. Nothing has happened?

So, my crisps being missing from my cupboard and there being an identical empty bag on the floor is just pure coincidence is it?

ACE. You're talking about the crisps.

She's talking about the crisps!

> (*As* **PAIGE** *talks,* **ACE** *moves themself away from* **ANT** *and out of danger.*)

PAIGE. *My* crisps Ace. Not *the* crisps. I don't mean to be a bitch here but it's the one thing I ask you not to touch. I feel weird that you can't respect that. This really isn't like a, what's mine is yours scenario.

ANT. Well...

PAIGE. Shut up Anthony.

ACE. I am genuinely sorry. I was going to replace them today but you're back early.

PAIGE. This is so awkward.

ANT. It's really not that a big a deal, in comparison to/

ACE. *(Shouting.)* It is a big deal Ant! You're so insensitive! Ignore him. You're totally right, I massively messed up and – I'm so selfish, sorry. I really need to work to repair your trust.

PAIGE. That is how I feel yeah.

ACE. I get you and again, I am so sorry.

> *(**PAIGE** heads to the kitchen.)*

I feel sick.

> *(**ACE** is throwing on clothes. They notice that they now have full furry legs, soft and brown with white spots. They panic.)*

ANT. Do you think we could –

ACE. Let me be really, super clear here. I don't want you, not ever again, not interested. Go in there and enjoy breakfast with your girlfriend and please keep your mouth shut – because if she finds out then we both have to leave and I have nowhere else to go. Nowhere Ant.

Don't screw me over. Please.

ANT. We have to do what's right.

ACE. No – no, no, no, no, no, no – no.

> *(**PAIGE** is back.)*

PAIGE. Ace do you mind if we have the living room to ourselves?

ACE. Was just about to suggest that. I'll get out your way.
Have a great day guys.

> (**ACE** *reluctantly leaves, eyeballing* **ANT** *with
> desperate eyes.*)

Ten

(**ACE** *is at the edge again.*)

(*They inspect their new furry legs anxiously. They drag a razor over themselves but it won't shift.*)

(*Ranting to themselves they thrash about.*)

(*They nibble on a branch.*)

(*They blow a few sad notes on their pan pipes.*)

(*They worry.*)

(*As it gets darker they hear the distant tranquil sound of a stream. It is calming and alluring.*)

(*They edge closer.*)

(*The smoke puffs billow upwards.*)

(*The distant sound of laughter and applause.*)

(*They step over in to the forest.*)

(*A shadowy figure comes forward taking them by surprise.*)

DOE. You coming in?

(**ACE** *freaks and leaps back over to the edge.*)

Okay...

Eleven

*(The house. **ACE** nervously enters the living room. **PAIGE** and **ANT** are sat on the sofa.)*

PAIGE. We can both make more of an effort, that's *both* of us though, not just on me.

ANT. I'm saying I'll put more effort in, that was my point.

PAIGE. Yes and I'm agreeing with you, idiot.

ACE. Can I come in?

PAIGE. Of course, sorry, were you wanting to go to bed?

Anthony we should go up, it's late.

ACE. You don't have to/

PAIGE. Anthony, come on.

Night Ace.

ACE. Night.

*(**ANT** gets up to leave, he meets **ACE** at the door, they linger on each other for a moment.)*

ANT. She doesn't know.

ACE. Thank you.

ANT. ...

(He leaves.)

ACE. Thank fuck.

(They flop on sofa.)

This is going to be the culmination of thirteen sofas worth of people pleasing. You are about to see my finest work.

(A montage of the ultimate fawning to **PAIGE** *across several days.)*

(1. Plumping pillows and smoothing the seat before she sits on the sofa. Bit weird.)

(2. Soothing panpipe tunes whilst she does a face-mask*.)

(3. **ACE** *hides/shrinks themselves to take up as little space as possible but can clearly still be seen.)*

ACE. Ignore me, I'm not even here, the lounge is all yours.

(4. Keeping **PAIGE***'s wine glass topped up and listening to her bitch about her work.)*

PAIGE. She was trying to say that the tobacco and white musk candle should be called fag hag – and I was like, is this the early '00s hun? Are you Lily Allen now?

*(***ACE** *fake laughs hard at the story,* **PAIGE** *is oblivious and pleased with being so funny.)*

(5. Putting out her washing.)

Oh great! So good of you to do that.

ACE. We're all friends here – I don't mind – and I don't touch the crotches, just to be respectful.

(6. **ACE** *leaps and frolics, with a huge grin, a perfect picture of gentle and sweet.)*

(7. **ACE** *avoids* **ANT***.)*

---

* A licence to produce *Faun* does not include a performance licence for any third-party or copyrighted music. Licensees should create an original composition or use music in the public domain. For further information, please see the Music and Third-Party Materials Use Note on page iii.

ANT. I feel like you're avoiding me.

ACE. Not at all. You know I like spending time with you. I'm just...busy.

ANT. *(Knows it's a fawn.)* Whatever.

> *(8. **ACE** paints a portrait of **ANT** and **PAIGE**, spins it round to reveal the pair inside a giant love heart.)*

> *(9. **ACE** walks past **PAIGE** doing yoga and gently corrects her downward dog.)*

PAIGE. You don't need to do that.

ACE. You deserve to feel the full stretch.

> *(10. **ANT** stops **ACE**.)*

ANT. This has to stop.

ACE. Don't know what you mean. Excuse me I've just got to check the oven.

ANT. Wait, listen. I'm trying to make it work with Paige but I can't do it without being honest with her.

ACE. You're a good person Ant. You're one of the best. It was me who messed up, don't lose what you have because I'm an idiot.

ANT. That isn't/

ACE. WHO WANTS CAKE!?

> *(11. **ACE** cooks an elaborate dish with tonnes of bowls and utensils. Flour flies about the place. **ACE** produces a giant croque-en – bouche and presents it to a bewildered **PAIGE**.)*

PAIGE. What is that?

ACE. It's for you. Take it. I made it for you. Enjoy it.

(**PAIGE** *takes the croque-en-bouche with a smile and leaves.*)

(**ACE** *alone and exhausted begins to kick and thrash around, head flailing, frustration, stress, rage.*)

(*They lift their top to reveal a full fluffy belly, brown with white spots just like their legs.*)

No, no, no, NO! I haven't got time for this right now.

(*Back to reality.*)

PAIGE. Still up for dinner tonight? I was thinking we could try that new/

ANT. I took an extra shift at work.

PAIGE. Oh.

(**PAIGE** *leaves, they clearly aren't working things out.*)

ANT. You look stressed, you okay?

ACE. All good. Have you got any old t-shirts you don't want by any chance? I need something baggy.

ANT. What?

ACE. Never mind. I'll check the charity boxes in the hall.

ANT. That's not charity donations, it's G's stuff. She's moving out.

ACE. What? When?

ANT. I've been trying to tell you but you're avoiding me. She's depressed, she's going back home.

ACE. Isn't she like thirty?

ANT. And? She's doing what she needs to do.

ACE. Yeah, sorry.

ACE. **I'm so gunna take her room!**

I'll be so sad to see her go.

ANT. Will you?

ACE. **No! I will literally shove her out the door.**

Yeah. But – I could take her room

ANT. Terrible idea.

ACE. I need a room Ant. Really badly.

ANT. We would sort of need someone who could pay for it.

ACE. I could pay *something* for it, maybe we could work out an income-based split?

ANT. Are you seriously asking me to pay more for you to permanently live here, are you mad?

ACE. It's perfect. Surely you can see it from my point of view.

ANT. And you can't see it from mine?

ACE. Genuinely, no.

ANT. This is messing me up man.

ACE. I'll do the cooking and the cleaning and stuff. I'll do whatever you guys need.

ANT. That would make it even weirder.

ACE. It wouldn't be any different to how it is now Ant. The only difference is that I'd have a room again. I wouldn't be in your way as much. This works.

ANT. Not for Paige it doesn't.

ACE. I'm sorry for what happened. We made a massive mistake, but you guys have made it work. What happened between us is a truth that she doesn't need to hear.

ANT. It was a mistake to you then yeah?

We haven't spoken so I didn't know.

You can take the room – I'll speak to Paige.

> *(He leaves.* **ACE** *leaps about in celebration, punching the air.)*

Twelve

(The house. **ACE** *is presenting* **PAIGE** *with the plan for the evening.)*

ACE. **You can't go wrong with cheap ingredients for a fancy meal and a big grin.**

Okay, I've got fancy ass fish cakes, a bag of salad that's like rocket and other posh leaves. I've got your favourite crisps and dips. And there's no Anthony this evening so no double dips in the hummus.

Did Ant talk to you about G's room and about me maybe having it? If you needed any more persuading that I am an ideal housemate, I've got another pan pipe cover down.

*(***PAIGE*** *empties the contents of the bag onto the floor without a care.)*

PAIGE. We talked yeah. I don't want your food. I want you out my house. You don't live here anymore.

(It sinks in. It can only be that she knows.)

ACE. **Shit**.

He told you?

PAIGE. He did. You can get your stuff together and leave now.

ACE. What about Ant?

PAIGE. What, you want to take him with you?

ACE. No, sorry –

I'm begging you, I will do anything. You're putting me on the street Paige.

PAIGE. You did it with my boyfriend! What's happening is all down to you.

ACE. You can't throw me out, I seriously have nowhere else to go.

PAIGE. You know what the most annoying thing is – *I'm* the one who got hurt and lied to but I'm still labelled the evil bitch who throws you out. *I'm* still the bad guy.

ACE. Can we talk about it? Please?

PAIGE. Why? Because boys will be boys. Or are you hoping that your situation makes you untouchable? Because let me be clear, you made a choice.

ACE. I'm so sorry.

PAIGE. No you aren't. People who are sorry don't lie for weeks on end. People who are sorry tell the truth.

ACE. Can we go for a walk and please talk this through? I'm happy to buy drinks?

PAIGE. You're right, I should absolutely offer a neutral ground for you to gaslight and manipulate me.

ACE. No, that's not it. I wouldn't. I know that you're angry but let me just say – people make mistakes.

PAIGE. I know that. But actions have consequences, nothing about your life gives you a free pass.

ACE. I'm not asking for a free pass, I'm asking for empathy, this is more complicated for me.

PAIGE. Oh, empathy! Because I'm a girl, right? I'm meant to just suck it up like its normal and think myself lucky that I've even got a man interested in me. Have him cry on my lap and say it meant nothing, he's sorry – and to feel sorry for you and be a good nurturer and let you stay. Shall I just light a sympathy and forgiveness scented candle for us. Make us a tea and cry about how it's probably my fault. Unfortunately for you two, I'm not that girl. I have a zero-tolerance policy when it comes to protecting my energy and my heart. You can go now. You can leave.

ACE. I'm different…

PAIGE. Oh my God are you about to say *not all men?*

ACE. No because I'm not a cis-man.

PAIGE. You sure as hell acted like one. And let's be real here, the misogyny club doesn't require you to show your birth certificate.

ACE. Paige please. I can't be perfect!

PAIGE. Perfect? No, I didn't expect you to be. But eating my crisps is one thing, eating my boyfriend is another, isn't it – It's a complete betrayal of trust.

ACE. **She'll let me stay, she just needs to get this off her chest. I'd know if I'd overstayed my welcome, I'd know before she did.**

I will do anything, seriously anything, I'll make sure we're never home at the same time or massage you, I give amazing massa –

> (**ACE** *reaches* **PAIGE***'s shoulders but sees two cloven hooves instead of hands.*)

What the actual f/

PAIGE. /You need to get out. Nothing you do will fix this. You can go now.

> (**PAIGE** *throws their stuff at them.*)

ACE. **Shit!**

> (**ACE** *grabs the bag and is gone.*)

Thirteen

(The edge.)

*(**ACE** is alone with their IKEA bag and is now a full-blown Faun. A half human, half baby deer combo. They have fawned so hard that they have fully faun-ed. It's a lot, ears, nubs, furry legs, furry body and two cloven hooves.)*

*(**ACE** picks up their IKEA bag and heads to their Mum's house. The doorway appears, religious adornments hang on it. The bin is overflowing with things. We don't pay attention to what's in there just yet.)*

(They knock.)

ACE. Mum?

I've got nowhere to go Mum, can I come in?

I'm scared. Please.

(They reach out to knock again and spot the bin, they see that it is full of big boxes filled with their things, a mixture of childhood objects, teenage outfit mistakes and junk.)

(Silently they sift through, taking one or two sentimental bits. Stuffing them in to the IKEA bag.)

Would be a bit heavy to take all of it.

Bye then things.

Bye then mum.

*(**ACE** picks up their bag and slowly leaves.)*

Fourteen

*(The edge. **ACE** stands staring in to the forest. There is nowhere else to go.)*

(They step in to it.)

*(Nervously they find a little spot to set up camp. The IKEA bag becomes a make-shift tent. As they work, **DOE** appears. An intimidating figure, they look cool, very much a human but with the **DOE** like features of someone who has grown from one who used to fawn, in to a confident, comfortable place.)*

ACE. *(Navigating around them.)* Excuse me, sorry.

Oh, is this your patch? Shit, sorry.

DOE. Wow you really went all in.

ACE. The tent? It's just an IKEA bag I've turned upside down.

DOE. I wasn't talking about the tent.

ACE. ...

I don't want any trouble, I'll just pack up and get out your way.

DOE. Do you know where you are?

ACE. Your bit of floor I think.

DOE. This is the Queer Forest babes, nobody owns space here.

ACE. Right. Sorry.

DOE. Wow.

Have you looked at me yet?

ACE. Not aggressively no! God no. I made sure to keep my eyes down to avoid conflict.

DOE. Hi.

>*(They look.)*

ACE. Oh shit. I mean hi, sorry. Hi, not shit.

DOE. Doe.

ACE. A deer?

DOE. Let's not do that. And you are?

ACE. Antlers-uh-Ace-sorry-I'm Ace.

DOE. Ciggy?

ACE. No thanks – no offence.

DOE. Mind if I?

ACE. No, God no. Have as many as you need. Have three at the same time? Do people do that? I bet *you* could!

>*(**DOE** smokes. **ACE** takes them in.)*

You're pulling all this off much better than I am.

DOE. Yes. I am.

ACE. …

DOE. Out of places to stay are we?

ACE. Yeah…I fucked up.

DOE. I'll leave you to it then. I'll find you tomorrow.

ACE. You can have this spot, I can/

DOE. You're welcome to stay as long as you need Ace.

But if you've recently taken up the panpipes, they are banned. They confuse the owls – they get violent.

>*(**DOE** casually leaves.)*

ACE. What time should I – oh excuse me, where will I find you –

Oh.

(Relief.) huh.

> *(Alone,* **ACE** *sits.)*
>
> *(This is the first time we see them calm.)*
>
> *(We hear a stream, wind through leaves, the sounds of peace.)*
>
> *(***ACE** *sleeps.)*
>
> *(When they wake* **DOE** *is sat next to them.)*

Agh! Sorry not agh, not a bad agh, you just made me jump – not in a bad way – my fault, not yours. Morning, need me to move?

> *(***DOE** *signals for him to be quiet.)*

DOE. No offence but I don't like to chat until *after* my morning cigarette.

ACE. *(Whispered.)* So should I move or/

> *(***DOE** *shushes them.)*
>
> *(***ACE** *takes the time to look at* **DOE***, a clear queer elder and clearly someone who can relate.)*
>
> *(***DOE** *has finished their cigarette.)*

DOE. Go on then.

> *(***ACE** *word vomits at a million miles an hour.)*

ACE. Are you like me then? Is everyone in here – well, furry and stuff? Do you have nubs? Because yours look like antlers, but – actually do they ever itch? like when you're angry and stuff, mine get so itchy. Have you got any tips on how to hide the cloven hooves? I figured long sleeves might work but that could get hot in the summer/

    (**DOE** *gestures for them to be quiet.*)

DOE. Why would you need a long sleeve t-shirt here?

ACE. Sorry.

DOE. Why would you need a long sleeve t-shirt here?

ACE. Oh no I heard. I was just apologising – sorry.

DOE. Wow!

Let's take this from the top then. Stand up and stretch out a bit.

Look in the water there, go on. Go on. A proper look, don't cheat. What do you see?

ACE. I honestly don't kn/

DOE. /Take a minute, do you see anyone rushing you?

    (**ACE** *looks, properly for the first time.*)

ACE. A faun.

DOE. A faun. And this is a forest. Relax yeah.

ACE. Relax, got it.

    (*A beat.*)

Not sure why I'm a fucking faun though!

SORRY! Sorry about that – overwhelmed there for a minute. Hope *you're* okay.

DOE. That would be why.

ACE. Sorry?

That was a question sorry not a sorry sorry – sorry.

DOE. How can you not see it? That is wild. Most people just peep in the stream and it clicks.

Look, let me spell this out for you. You're in a crisis, agreed? Everyone's options in a crisis are fight, flight, freeze or fawn. This, all this, it's a literal manifestation of how you behave. It's your survival tactic. And thank fuck you came here babe – you look just about ready to explode from all that fawning. – and if you did, you'd probably apologise *as* you popped into a gooey mess. *(Makes the noise of an explosion and does an impression.)* Oh gosh, sorry!

ACE. That does sound like me...

DOE. But here you are. Would you look at that. You're a faun who needs to be in a forest. And the forest will provide.

ACE. Provide what?

DOE. De-fawning babe.

ACE. Oh. Oh, I see.

Uh, I didn't know this was one of those places, and I thought that you were – you know – But I, I don't want to get caught up in any de-transition bullshit – freedom of speech and all that, I know. But also like, freedom to call people out for being stupid.

DOE. Excuse you?

ACE. I'm not here to fight, honestly. It's not even a discussion, my transness is, it's all good, it's great, better than great, and normal, also, very, very normal.

DOE. I said de-fawn not de-transition.

ACE. And I am politely saying, no thanks.

DOE. Good to know.

ACE. If I wasn't at the lowest point in my life right now, I'd talk to you about how wrong your opinions are but/

DOE. Oh, would you?

ACE. I just can't take on that emotional labour at the moment, sorry. All the best, best wishes to you.

DOE. You finished?

ACE. Yeah.

DOE. De-fawning is removing your faun elements. No one gives a shit that you're trans.

Feel free to leave though babe.

ACE. I am so sorry.

DOE. Stop apologising! Stop. You thought I held shitty beliefs and you called me out, why did you apologise? Seriously though, why?

ACE. …

DOE. BECAUSE YOU ARE FAWNING! UGH! I'm gunna need some help here. Follow me.

(**DOE** *leads* **ACE** *away.*)

Fifteen

(**DOE** *brings* **ACE** *to see* **PLANT**.)

DOE. Plant Ace, Ace Plant.

ACE. ...Hello.

(**PLANT** *waves.*)

Woah.

DOE. I know, I know, magical forests are usually reserved for cis-het fairy-tales but not this one, okay?

One sec yeah.

(*They take* **PLANT** *aside.*)

This kid arrived yesterday and they're not getting it. And look at them.

(**PLANT** *shrugs.*)

We're going to need to do our thing.

(**PLANT** *is nonchalant.*)

What's your problem?

(**PLANT** *gestures.*)

It's not all about me, we do it fifty fifty.

(**PLANT** *gestures.*)

Okay, fine, yes, it is a bit about me. But what's wrong with that? I haven't failed in getting someone to a de-fawning ceremony in forever. And I ain't about to break that streak.

Do the thing.

(**PLANT** *gestures.*)

DOE. Ace come here.

   Plant here sees the past

ACE. Isn't that just...memory.

DOE. Other people's past.

ACE. What like a time traveller?!

DOE. Like a past-seeing plant, just roll with it.

>   *(There is a conjuring of the past from* **DOE**
>   *and* **PLANT**.*)*
>
>   *(Then.)*
>
>   *(***PLANT** *passes them a small sofa that fits in*
>   *their hand.)*

ACE. Wait, is this, is this sofa number one?

DOE. Did sofa number one have an ashtray?

ACE. No.

DOE. It does now. *(They tap their cigarette.)*

>   *(***ACE** *puts it down.)*
>
>   *(***PLANT** *is not pleased, they throw the tiny*
>   *sofa back.)*

ACE. How did you know about sofa number one?

DOE. Tell me what it was like?

ACE. You can see the past, look yourselves.

DOE. Trust me, you need to say it.

ACE. Ugh, it was in my cousin's place. It was covered in
   matted cat hair and I looked like I had permanent pink
   eye – but it was fine.

DOE. Oh it was fine, oh okay sure. I fully believe you, it's not like you're standing in a forest as a faun – because that would *definitely* mean it wasn't fine.

Oh wait...

ACE. Okay, not fine, too much cat hair.

DOE. Did they not have a hoover? Lint roller?

ACE. I thought it would be rude to ask.

> (**PLANT** *slaps* **ACE** *with a leaf hand, gently but enough to shock them. The forest disapproves of this behaviour.*)

Ow! What the/

> (**PLANT** *smiles and offers another sofa.* **ACE** *is wary until they recognise it.*)

No way, sofa number six. This one was mad comfy. Usually I have to curl up and bend my knees but on this one I could stretch all the way out, it was all squishy like a hug.

DOE. (*Sarcastic.*) Ooh how many colours does it come in?

ACE. I didn't buy it, sorry. But if you give me one second I can definitely find it online for you.

> (*Another leaf whacks* **ACE** *around the face.*)

Ow, why?

DOE. No fawning! You're in the middle of an existential crisis babe and you want to smear those hooves all over a phone screen so that I can find a sofa?

E-nough of that. Thank you.

ACE. I honestly don't see how looking at tiny sofas from my past is going to help me here.

DOE. Oooh feisty, that's better.

Tell me more.

ACE. I don't want to – it wasn't exactly great. They asked me to clean in exchange for staying there. I felt like a servant.

DOE. Their fault or yours?

ACE. Mine.

> (**PLANT** *slaps* **ACE**, *a comical amount.*)

STOP SLAPPING ME DUDE!

> (**PLANT** *shrugs.*)

DOE. You said it was *your* fault.

ACE. I mean they shouldn't have asked I guess but/

> (**PLANT** *preps for a whack.*)

What's your problem?

DOE. No fawning! What do you *actually* think? It's okay to say. Nothing's going to be taken away from you Ace.

ACE. That it was shitty for them to ask me to clean their shit.

> (**PLANT** *lowers their hand, a little disappointed.*)

DOE. Better.

ACE. Of course I didn't think it was right, but I didn't have much choice.

> (**PLANT** *conjures a huge sofa from the forest.*)

DOE. Uh oh, here it comes.

ACE. No.

> (**PLANT** *and* **DOE** *sit.*)

DOE. Yep, your Mums.

ACE. Why would you do that –

DOE. Truth hurts. This ain't no walk in the park babe – because it's a forest for starters.

ACE. I know it's a forest, you keep reminding me! You have no right to go digging about in my past, judging my decisions. You don't even know me.

DOE. You came to us remember.

ACE. Of course I remember, I literally had nowhere else to go.

(**PLANT** *pats the sofa for* **ACE** *to join.*)

DOE. Not now plant, read the room yeah.

ACE. I'm sorry, I should never have come here.

DOE. You don't need to apologise Ace, that's what I'm trying to show you.

ACE. It's just who I am, you don't understand.

DOE. Of course I do. What do you think this is, fancy-fucking-dress?

Your Mum's sofa is here because that's where it started. I understand that. You get me? Mine was prickets that grew first, was it the same for you? But you have to understand that prickets grow into antlers.

ACE. I don't want antlers, no offence, sorry. I just want my life back. This is all just weird, and I've got enough weird going on right now thanks! I just want it to stop.

(*They leave.*)

(**PLANT** *gestures.*)

DOE. Nah. Let them go. I think they'll work it out.

(**DOE** *leaves.* **ACE** *returns and snatches up* **PLANT**.)

Sixteen

*(***ACE***'s mums living room. ***ACE*** sits on her sofa with ***PLANT*** alongside.)*

ACE. **I know what you're thinking. What the fuck are they doing in their mum's house. But I'm thinking that all this** *(Gestures faun parts.)* **started here so it can end here.**

No money for a succulent so this guy will have to do.

(Calling off.)

I think it's some sort of Calathea or Monstera maybe. Anyway, I thought it would look good in here.

Nothing looks good in here, it hasn't been decorated since 2002.

Do you want a hand in the kitchen Mum?

(No response.)

I'll take that as a no.

Cool.

She kept the tea pots look – gross.

I was wondering if we could talk – about...everything.

(No response.)

She went straight in there after she opened the door...hopefully she's not poisoning my coffee.

I'd like to apologise.

Then she can do a big fat apology to me.

I'm sorry for anything I've done to upset you.

Which is nothing by the way.

ACE. Don't worry about chucking my stuff out, I'm not annoyed.

I'm furious.

We all do things we regret when emotions run high.

The pronouns aren't make or break either, I get that it's hard.

(No response.)

(To **PLANT.***)*

What are you looking at?

You're a gift. Perk up a bit.

(A long wait.)

I'm going in there.

(They check the kitchen and return.)

(They flop.)

She left. Backdoor's open.

*(***PLANT*** comforts* **ACE.***)*

It wouldn't have made any difference would it? I could have apologised a thousand times and it wouldn't have made a difference.

Fawned myself in to a faun and it made no difference.

I don't know who I am if I don't do this.

*(***PLANT*** gives* **ACE** *a teapot.)*

Don't touch those they're collectibles – and they've had turds in.

(Shifting.)

They've had turds in.

ACE. Not very fawn like to desecrate your Mum's tea pots.

Not very fawn like at all.

That's who I was. That's who I am, under all this. So if I'm more like that again then –

> *(They swing* **PLANT** *around smashing the place.)*

That felt so fucking good!

> *(Expecting a miraculous transformation.)*

So, this should all be going anytime soon. I fixed it, right?

Any moment now. Bye bye nubs. Buh-bye, shed, shed, shed. Whenever you're ready, off you fuck.

(To **PLANT**.*)* Why isn't it going?

> *(They look to* **PLANT**. **PLANT** *gives a look of – you know there's work still to do.)*

Oh Fuck it.

> *(They stomp off.)*

Seventeen

*(The Queer Forest. **ACE** stomps back in with **PLANT** in tow. **DOE** sits smoking as always.)*

ACE. Doe! I'm back. As you can see, because I'm stood here.

DOE. You stole from the forest. You stole Plant from the forest.

I should kick your ass.

ACE. Yeah, I stole Plant, yeah, I did. Because I'm a flawed human being and that's what I want to be.

DOE. Excuse you?

ACE. Yeah excuse me, I've got work to do. I'm de-fawning, down to the bare bones. All this is going. I'm going to change the shit out of my insides to get this crap off my outsides. You with me?

DOE. And what's changed exactly?

ACE. I smashed up my Mums teapots.

DOE. That's a new one.

ACE. When I first left I think I thought I could fix it by being...better...or softer or something.

I thought I could survive it if I stayed small, stayed pleasing, stayed smiling and polite –

DOE. Because if your mum can turn on you, then anyone can.

ACE. You do get it.

DOE. It's almost like that's what I was trying to tell you...

ACE. Will you have me back then?

DOE. I'll think about it.

(**DOE** *smokes a few drags.*)

DOE. I've thought about it. Yes, you can stay.

But you steal from here again and I'll rip your eyes out. Got it?

ACE. Bit extreme.

DOE. Got it?!

ACE. Got it.

DOE. Good.

First things first babe you need to learn how to take up space again, yeah?

ACE. I can do that.

(**ACE** *slowly starts to walk about, it develops in to a swagger, the swinging of arms, it's a bit pathetic but an endearing attempt.*)

How's this?

DOE. Not what I meant.

ACE. Oh.

DOE. This is the Queer Forest. Use it.

You want to run – run

You want to scream – do it.

You want to stomp?

ACE. I do like that yeah.

DOE. Stomp then!

Eat where you like, shit where you need, piss all up a tree for all I care.

ACE. I probably won't –

DOE. Come on.

>*(DOE leads ACE through a
>Disney-esque montage of letting loose and
>being unashamedly what you are.)*

>*(They scream – it's like a roar of pain and
>satisfaction all at once.)*

ACE. IT'S SO GOOD TO BE LOUD AND NOT CARE!

DOE. Keep going then!

>*(ACE screams again. A scream that calls out
>to the ACE from the past and forward to the
>ACE's of the future. It exhausts them for a
>moment.)*

>*(DOE begins to deer stomp but to a beat,
>so that its less about stress and more about
>freedom.)*

Feel that? We're all wild creatures at heart Ace. But
those mammal instincts can get crushed by this little
bitch of a world we live in. You get me?

ACE. Yes.

DOE. If you push all your thoughts and feelings down
all the damn time then you're nothing but a playdoh
person for other people to mould.

ACE. I need to be wild.

DOE. Wiiild.

>*(ACE is re-ignited – he joins in the stomp.)*

ACE. Authentic.

DOE. I like it!

ACE. I want to loosen up.

DOE. Let it happen.

ACE. Oh it's going to.

DOE. I see you. Lean in to it, don't hold back now.

ACE. Fuck it!/

DOE. /You've got this.

ACE. DEER DANCE!

> *(A deer dance happens. It is full of everything that **ACE** has been holding in. It is unashamedly everything that **ACE** is, good and bad. It's raw and beautiful, sad and stunning, elating and explosive. It's so queer!)*

> *(They stop for a breather.)*

Hungry?

DOE. Does a bear shit in the woods?

> *(**ACE** throws **DOE** a branch, they both destroy it and gorge on leaves.)*

You pissed on a tree yet?

ACE. I really don't want to.

DOE. Why?

Worried what people will think of you?

ACE. No. It just sounds gross!

DOE. GOOD! If that's your truth then stick to it! Don't do it just because I said.

> *(**ACE** looks in to the stream.)*

ACE. I feel huge, look at me. HUGE!

I want to headbutt something.

DOE. Let's not tip into toxic masculinity. Plant *will* slap you.

ACE. I want to re-introduce myself.

I'm Ace.

DOE. Am I meant to act like we just met yeah? That's what we're doing?

(**ACE** *nods.*)

Hi Ace, I'm Doe. Ciggy?

ACE. No.

DOE. Mind if I?

ACE. Go for it.

DOE. I'll miss you a bit you know.

(**ACE** *is surprised.*)

What? I always miss the grads.

ACE. I'm not going yet.

(*The distant sound of music and drums*.)

DOE. It's time. You've got to grasp it with both hands Ace.

You deserve a quieter life, a Sunday hungover – feeling like death, in a bed, your bed, even if it's a single, it'll be perfect.

You need to go out and earn your average twenty-something regrets. Make those light-hearted mistakes that crush your world for an hour or two but are then just laughed off, because you can afford for them to just be a part of life, not the end of everything.

Let me put it this way, if you stay this stressed you are going to age. It will wrinkle your skin.

---

* A licence to produce *Faun* does not include a performance licence for any third-party or copyrighted music. Licensees should create an original composition or use music in the public domain. For further information, please see the Music and Third-Party Materials Use Note on page iii.

ACE. Good to know.

DOE. You'll look like a sad little ball bag.

ACE. Wow.

I will come back though. To see you.

DOE. You better not. I don't give the same advice twice.

> (**ACE** *nods.*)

> (**DOE** *grabs* **ACE** *for a hug.*)

> (*The sound of the ceremony builds, its calling.*)

Your ceremony awaits babe. You're going to love this bit.

ACE. I never asked you what actually –

> (**DOE** *has gone.*)

Happens…

Eighteen

(The forest. The de-fawning ceremony. A loud and dazzling spectacle that fills the space and includes the audience. A celebration with a huge amount of sparkle and wonder.)

*(**STAG** is the master of ceremonies, full of quick wit and charisma. They enter to a loud track, something iconic to the LGBTQ+ community, something camp and queer that speaks to generations.)*

STAG. Well hello there, take a moment, take all this in. You're only human.

I'm Stag and I'm your host for this evening's main event!

Okay my polite little potatoes, let's turn that volume right up. I want to hear you *cheer* for this god like, horny deer, so I'll say it again – I'm Stag and I'm your host for this evening's main event!

They live! Well good evening and hello to you, to you and you and you. Hello to my ladies, let me hear you! Peppered about, good. My gents? Always, obvious where you are – no offence. And my gentlethems? Yes, yes, always a good turnout. And last but not least my mascs and femmes? *(If a whoop.)* Always one whooper, we hear you and we see you.

You're here, Stag's here so let's de-fawn some deer.

Yes, my wee squirrels! We are here tonight to big up those who are in need. The queers with fears. The bi's who need to cut their toxic ties. The gays in their appeasing phase. The lesbians who are not tres biens. The pans who need to know they can. The nonbinary fineries who need help to shine-ery and the trans who are feeling closed up like clams.

STAG. This is a graduation for those who have been diminishing themselves around others, keeping their wee light under a bushel, but who are now ready to shake it off. We must grow my broad beans, allow me to fertilise your soils – with confidence, you cheeky things – *(Pointing someone out.)* I saw how you looked at me there, it's been noted, I'll find you later.

Now can I get a – WE CAN?

> *(They encourage the audience to shout, we can.)*

Can I get a – WE MUST?

> *(They encourage the audience to shout, we must.)*

Can I get a – double gin and diet tonic? – seriously.

And can I get a WE WILL.

> *(The audience will hopefully shout we will...)*

We can, we must, we will be scooping up fawners by the bucket load and washing them clean of their people pleasing sins.

No one is immune mes petit pois. Fawning can befall anyone of us. In particular us queers. And yes, I myself am of that persuasion. If you hadn't guessed that already then – good for you! One should never assume.

Now what's a ceremony without testimony, am I right? Who's first? We're shy? That's okay. I'll kick us off.

Picture the scene, its 2005, X-Factor's on, I've got a Blue WKD in hand and a Christina Aguilera poster staring me down, when suddenly – BAM – I've overplucked my eyebrows – to fit in – if you lived through "the pluckening" you'll understand.

But enough about me, how about you?

(Here **STAG** *is free to talk to audience members individually, getting to know people and pulling out stories of their fawning behaviour. This should be funny but the conversations should never put people down or humiliate them for the laugh.)*

STAG. Enough about you, let's get back to me. I stand before you this evening having done hundreds of de-fawning ceremonies and having sent hundreds of people of all types, ages and persuasions out of this forest with a – *don't try me* – attitude and the dewy glow of a five – step skin care routine.

So, who's next?

Who amongst us has nubs, of the velvety kind? Who here has small, twitch prone ears? Who amongst you has a furry belly – now I should stress at this point that bears and some otters could get confused, yours is hair babes, I'm talking fur!

ACE. ME! HELLO! – not sure why I'm shouting.

STAG. We love a keen one, hello there, come up, tell me your name.

ACE. *(Nervous and a tad too loud.)* I'm Ace – I'm a massive faun!

STAG. Can't de-fawn without fauns, so don't you worry about that.

Ace everyone, let's hear it!

(**DOE** *encourages the crowd to get behind* **ACE.***)*

Welcome faun child, feel no shame, you are accepted here.

(**ACE** *looks up at* **STAG**, *a future version of themselves, so confident and so beautiful. They are in awe.*)

STAG. As a community we will hold you – metaphorically, we respect boundaries.

Do you wish to be de-fawned?

ACE. Hell yes.

STAG. We use the healing powers of the queer stream.

One big DIP and you're done.

ACE. I don't swim, will that be a/

STAG. It's a dip dear child not a drowning.

A short, sharp, shock to the system.

You'll stand on the bank anxious and small then –

DIP!

You'll emerge empowered.

Happy?

ACE. Dip me, dip me good! I want to appear out that water like a shimmery mermaid – brand new and looking like an absolute ride.

STAG. We are washing away your fawning ways my dinky duckling, nothing more, nothing less. You are exactly as you should be, up and down.

Are you ready my tiny toe?

ACE. DIP ME!

STAG. Then we must have silence please.

(**STAG** *and* **DOE** *perform the ceremony song, it begins with the sound of the distant deep singing that* **ACE** *could hear earlier when at* *the edge*. It is both a bit funny and camp as well as soulful and enjoyable.)*

(The song ends and **ACE** *is gently led forwards.)*

STAG. Repeat after me.

(The following is call and response with **ACE**/ *the audience if they are rowdy.)*

I don't have to people please.

If someone expects me to, then I'll say – BITCH PLEASE!!

Louder! BITCH PLEASE!

BITCH PLLEEAASSEE!

It's time, all together now.

(They encourage the crowd to shout DIP and clap.)

DIP

DIP

DIP

DIP

(Boom, **ACE** *is dipped in the stream.)*

(A transformation.)

(They emerge once again, no more fur or ears. Their nubs turned to tiny glitter antlers.)

STAG. Another one tipped, dipped and stripped of fawning! Congratulations kid.

---

* A licence to produce *Faun* does not include a performance licence for any third-party or copyrighted music. Licensees should create an original composition or use music in the public domain. For further information, please see the Music and Third-Party Materials Use Note on page iii.

MUSIC PLEASE! AND DRINKS!

> *(Confetti cannons burst!)*

> *(Music and celebration.)*

> *(Hugs from* **DOE***.)*

ACE. I bloody did it.

DOE. You can thank me later.

ACE. Look at me! I'm back! Why don't you get dipped? It feels great.

DOE. I don't need to hide my past here babes, this is *our* space. And I look incredible.

ACE. Thanks for...everything.

DOE. Yeah, yeah, I'm the best, I know.

ACE. *(Realising what's on their head.)* Wait, I've still got these fucking things.

> *(Everything stops.)*

DOE. We just covered that. You're amongst your own Ace, let it be. And trust me on this, you cannot grow glitter antlers if you don't start with nubs!

STAG. GET THAT MUSIC BACK ON AND GET ME A GIN.

> *(Music and celebration resumes. Queers together – in that explosive, expansive way that only our shared experience can conjure. Every one of us should feel good.)*

> *(Dancing. A party.)*

> *(As the party rages.)*

> *(**ACE** steps back over into the edge.)*

Nineteen

(The edge. The Queer Forest gone in an instant. Now only the sound of a London street.)

(Their IKEA bag falls at their feet.)

*(**ACE** takes a breath. A distinct difference in who they are, a confidence.)*

ACE. Still Ace, still twenty-two, still Leo sun, still Aquarius moon, intuitive, creative...*not* a fawner.

Not yet a room renter. But a subletter. More than a sofa but not quite a rent, you know? Keep off the council tax, that's the trick.

I've got some more shifts at work, so if I give up Netflix and coffees from Pret then I'll be buying a two-bed new build in no time, according to the boomers...

Anyway,

This won't quite be a masterclass. I'm kind of new to it – no succulents and no sugar cubes.

Just me.

And a growing pair of glittery antlers.

(A doorbell appears and he presses it.)

*(A **BITCHY GAY** answers.)*

BITCHY GAY. Hi.

ACE. Hi, I'm Ace, I'm here to view the room.

BITCHY GAY. You're fifteen minutes late babe – bad start.

ACE. Sorry yeah, I –

*(**ACE** catches themselves fawning.)*

The tube was delayed. You know how it is.

BITCHY GAY. I get Ubers babe. I earn a lot of money. Anyway, come in – I guess – but wipe your feet and keep your voice down, Heather is on night shifts so we can't piss her off.

ACE. You know what – I'm good. Have a great day.

*(The **BITCHY GAY** and the doorbell fade.)*

(A new doorbell appears and they press it.)

(A cis-gender, very posh girl answers.)

POSH. Oh my gosh, look at you, you are so cute.

ACE. Hi, here to see the room.

POSH. You're even cuter than the photo. Also, also, also – I just want you to know that we have a friend Lyra, and she is a they now – yah, yah. She just came out with it last week – she was like – *fuck the patriarchy* – and we were like – *woooo!!* And we just think she is, sorry, *they* is so, so, brave.

ACE. Okay...

POSH. Yah, so we are allies now which is lush. And to know two of you is even more lush.

ACE. I'm not coming in.

POSH. Oh my gosh why? I've just ordered a rainbow flag for the window!

*(The doorbell and **POSH** fade.)*

(Another doorbell appears, they press it.)

*(**ANT** answers.)*

ANT. Ace?

ACE. Ant. Shit.

ANT. What are you doing here?

ACE. You have a room to sublet? Someone called Nia posted it?

ANT. Oh. I didn't know she'd –

ACE. Your girlfriend?

ANT. No.

ACE. Social and outgoing bar manager who loves food, video games and 80s pop ballads. Should have guessed it was you.

ANT. I wrote handsome and well hung but she must have deleted that bit.

ACE. Cool, well, good to see you –

ANT. It's good that you can afford a room.

ACE. It's a box room – as you know.

ANT. Yeah, mine too.

ACE. Oh. Cool.

ANT. You look more like, confident.

ACE. I am.

ANT. Suits you. Listen I'm sorry about all that stuff with Paige, I understand if you're pissed at me.

ACE. I am a bit yeah – but it's okay, it helped me find what I needed.

ANT. You okay?

ACE. You know what, I am actually.

ANT. Cool.

ACE. I should get going then. Try the next place.

ANT. No way, come in, it's getting dark and at least you know you're safe here.

> *(A light hits **ACE**, he glows in it.)*

You look incredible.

> *(**ACE** admires themselves. A stag shaped shadow hits the ground. Bold and strong.)*

ACE. I know.

> *(**ANT** opens the door and **ACE** steps in past him. He smiles, in love.)*

Milton Keynes UK
Ingram Content Group UK Ltd.
UKHW022148060624
443848UK00015BB/115